# The GREATEST Karate Fighter of All Time

To Kim, my wife and friend, and to my son, Cameron, and daughter, Kristina.

—J.L.

To Gina, my wife and partner, and to Cody and Tyler, my inspiring sons.

—J.B.

Joe Lewis & Jerry Beasley

# The GREATEST Karate Fighter of All Time

## Joe Lewis and His American Karate Systems

Paladin Press · Boulder, Colorado

**Also by Jerry Beasley:**

*In Search of the Ultimate Martial Art:*
*The Jeet Kune Do Experience*

*The Way of No Way:*
*Solving the Jeet Kune Do Riddle*

*"The Greatest Karate Fighter of All Time":*
*Joe Lewis and His American Karate Systems*
by Joe Lewis and Dr. Jerry Beasley

ISBN 0-87364-981-8
Printed in the United States of America

Published by Paladin Press, a division of
Paladin Enterprises, Inc., P.O. Box 1307,
Boulder, Colorado 80306, USA.
(303) 443-7250

Direct inquiries and/or orders to the above address.

# CONTENTS

# ACKNOWLEDGMENTS

The authors would like to thank Gina Beasley, who, as a professional editor, transformed the rough copy into a presentable manuscript. We constantly made changes, added new ideas, and revised the copy. She took the time, provided the encouragement, and, in the end, made final edits under the pressure of meeting the publication deadline. We owe her our gratitude.

Our thanks also are extended to Ric Anderton of Radford University (Radford, Va.), who provided many of the photographs, and to Jearl Sutherland and John Graden, who posed as sparring partners.

Thanks also to Jon Ford of Paladin Press, for always having a friendly tone and the willingness to take a chance on a new book idea.

# INTRODUCTION
## Going to the Source

**A** gifted athlete, Joe Lewis has won more prestigious titles, set more records, and instituted more innovations in competitive karate than any other individual or group in the history of martial arts in America. He has been inducted into 12 national and international halls of fame, including the most prestigious such organization, the *Black Belt* Hall of Fame, both as "Fighter of the Year" (1974) and as "Instructor of the Year" (1985). *Kick Illustrated* (now *Inside Karate*) called him the "Grandmaster of American Karate," and in 1983, *Karate Illustrated* selected a panel of America's top competitors (including Chuck Norris and world champion Bill "Superfoot" Wallace), who unanimously voted Lewis the title of "The Greatest Karate Fighter of All Time."

Joe Lewis began his training on Okinawa studying with three instructors: Eizo Shimabuku, Kinjo Chinsaku, and Seiyu Oyata. Although he received his black belt in shorin ryu, Lewis is an advocate of having no style. In the late 1960s, he trained extensively with Bruce Lee. The pairing of these two unique individuals has resulted in the advanced strategies for fighting exemplified in the innovative American full-contact karate/kickboxing, which electrified the karate world in the 1970s.

Lewis was a member of the 8th Marine Brigade, the first combat unit in Vietnam (1965). He was one of the first Americans to teach hand-to-hand combat in Vietnam, working with Recon. In

Vietnam, Joe found that, in battle, you quickly learn to discard anything that doesn't work. Upon his return to the United States in 1966, Joe won the first tournament he entered. The tournament was the prestigious U.S. National Championships, held in Washington, D.C., during which he used only two techniques: the reverse punch and the side kick. Yet he won every bout during the day-long event and only gave up a single point. He was that good.

After appearing on magazine covers and receiving the attention of every major martial arts publication, Lewis became disenchanted with non-contact karate. After all, he weighed just over 200 pounds and was made out of rock-hard, sinewy muscle. To deliver a technique to an opponent and have to pull it short was not exactly what Lewis had in mind; he was a fighter. In Vietnam he found that using only what works was the way of the true warrior. Now he wanted to apply this same spirit in sport competition.

As it turned out, Bruce Lee, Lewis' personal trainer from 1967–69, had developed a style called jeet kune do (JKD), which also emphasized using only what works. Lee often attended karate tournaments and stood by his prized pupil as Lewis won title after title. In 1968, Lewis began teaching the principles of jeet kune do in seminars across the country. Then, in 1970, he put it all together by creating the sport of American full-contact karate.

Referred to as kickboxing because the combatants wore boxing gear, the rules of full-contact karate were simple: you could hit your opponent with any fist or foot technique, as well as the knees, with as much power as you could muster. Unlike karate bouts in which the winner is judged to be the person who scores the most annoying taps to his opponent's body, full-contact meant just that—trying to take out the opponent with the fastest, most efficient means available. Here again, style means nothing and efficiency means everything.

After training in the realities of Vietnam, studying the effectiveness of Bruce Lee's jeet kune do, and applying those theories to his natural ability and proven competition record, Lewis had become an unstoppable force.

In 1970 and 1971, 10 of the top fighting champions of the day faced Lewis in full-contact competition. Each fighter hit the mat, knocked unconscious and completely defenseless in under two rounds. Once, in Texas, a giant of a man named Ed Daniels challenged Lewis. Daniels stood 6'8", weighed 280 pounds, and had known no equal among the tough Texas competitors. All this meant nothing to Joe Lewis, who, after receiving a vicious knee to the chest, proceeded to knock Daniels out with a right cross–left hook combination that sent Daniels to the emergency room and almost cost him his life.

With no opponents left to fight, Lewis retired from full-contact in 1971, only to be reunited with the sport in 1974 when he became the undisputed full-contact karate heavyweight champion of the world. With his title eventually retired, Lewis went on to star in two major films: *Jaguar Lives* and *Force Five*. His acting career was temporarily put on hold during the summer of 1982, when he traveled home to Knightdale, North Carolina, because of family illness.

The change from the fast-paced studios of Hollywood to the considerably more relaxed southern style of North Carolina had apparently sparked new instincts in the champ's competitive desires. Standing in his childhood home, where he had once lifted weights and dreamed of becoming a champion, Lewis, then 39, had done it all. He had traveled the globe for seminars, won every major title in his sport, and signed contracts amounting to more than $1 million in potential movie contracts. But could he still fight in the ring?

Working out daily in a local gym, Lewis decided to re-enter competition. True, he *was* 39. And as a movie star, he hadn't fought in more than seven years because he couldn't risk getting cut or disfigured for the camera. Now here he was, back in the ring again in a South Carolina coliseum filled with fight fans, many having made the trip just to see the living legend fight again. Did he still have it?

As his opponents found out that night, Lewis had never lost it. His superior martial arts knowledge, physical skills, and ring savvy had once again proven him more than a match for his competitors. Just as he had done more than 10 years earlier, he knocked his opponent out before the end of the third round.

As I write this, Joe is in his early 50s and is still fighting. For the past 15 years, he has been one of the most requested seminar performers in the world. An article in *Black Belt* magazine once noted that Lewis had completed 15 seminars in 15 days, each in a different city. He completes more than 100 seminars each year as eager fans gather to learn the secrets of the "Greatest Karate Fighter of All Time."

As this book's co-author, I am pleased to offer the first book ever penned regarding the Joe Lewis American Karate Systems (JLAKS). I have been a student of Lewis since 1982 and first heard about him back in 1968 when my instructor at the time, Whit Davis, kept telling us, "Strike and move! You've got to be mobile! Fight like Joe Lewis; he's always moving." I didn't know who Joe Lewis was at the time, but throughout my career as a professional martial artist I have been greatly influenced by those first few classes and by Lewis' systems. Without doubt, Joe Lewis and Bruce Lee are, in my mind, the two greatest martial artists of all time. Lee had the principles and Lewis put the principles to work.

In this book, I had only intended to organize a standard for teaching the Joe Lewis American Karate Systems. In the process of collecting information, I conducted extensive interviews and photo sessions with the champ over a 10-year period. In the end, I found that it would best satisfy his many thousands of fans if I presented, as much as possible, the information in his own words.

As I reviewed my notes, collected from countless hours of research and training in his systems, I began to play the tapes. I heard Joe talk about his dream as a youngster, first black belt, first tournament, and his amazing revelations on fighting and karate. So that the reader may feel as though he is actually being taught by the champ, I have arranged the book so that Joe himself teaches you. He is the source of much of the knowledge of martial arts that I now claim as my own. So here, in his own words, is the story of the "Greatest Karate Fighter of All Time."

—Jerry Beasley
Radford University

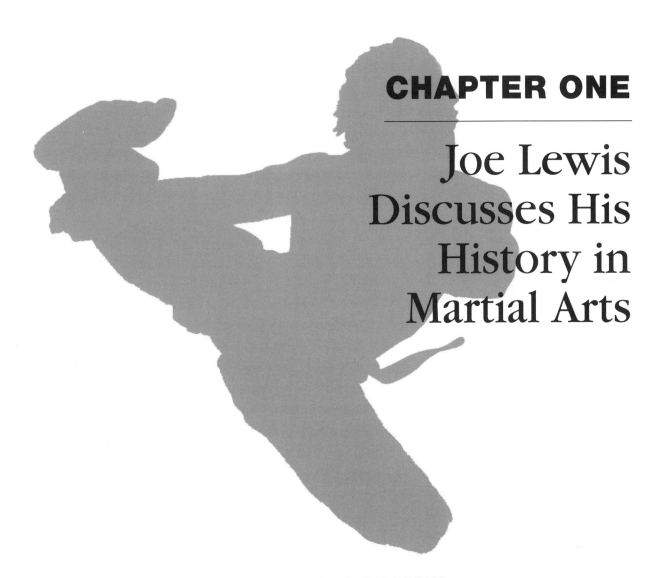

# CHAPTER ONE

# Joe Lewis Discusses His History in Martial Arts

## THE EARLY YEARS: THE DREAM

I was born on March 7, 1944, in Raleigh, North Carolina, but I grew up in both Knightdale and Raleigh. Both of my parents were teachers; my dad was a college professor and my mom taught in the public school system. My parents, my brothers, and I all lived on a big farm in Knightdale. When I was about 14 years old, I started playing around with weights and enjoyed doing hand stands and balancing acts for attention. I used to go into town to the YMCA, where I was impressed by a group of kids who were lifting weights and doing Olympic lifts, since I was always interested in being really muscular, strong, and fast. (My dream was to be the fastest man in the world. There was a kid going to Duke University, Dave Sim, who was studying to become a neurosurgeon or a brain surgeon. At one time, he actually was the fastest man in the world, but he blew it in the Olympic Games because he got off to a slow start and a little German kid beat him.) I wanted to be the greatest at something; I just hadn't decided what yet.

I would often go down to the magazine stands—I couldn't afford the magazines, but I'd look at the muscle mags—and dream of being very muscular like some of those guys. I liked Bill

Pearl and Reg Parks. Those kinds of guys were my idols. Once in a while, I'd see someone who had one muscle group that I liked, like Lou Delli, who had incredible deltoids, and Leroy Corbet, who had huge (21-inch) biceps. They would always talk about the squat-lifting movements that Paul Anderson could do. And then, after a while, someone would come along and blow away all the records.

My interest in weight lifting was strengthened when my brother made a little barbell (it weighed between 25 and 35 pounds) in shop. He brought the thing home and the end of it fell off the bar. I went downstairs and fixed it in the basement and started doing different movements. In about three weeks, my arms began to swell and soon became big. That got me hooked.

I made myself a makeshift barbell, too. I also took a five-gallon bucket, put a board on it, and did sit-ups and Vs. The plumbing and pipes downstairs came in handy as well, as I'd get up there and do chin-ups, pull-ups, all kinds of leg raises, and stuff like that. I'd also ride bikes in the hills in the middle of the night to build up my legs. I even started my own gym, which cost me absolutely nothing. I don't think my parents wanted me to lift weights because they thought I should use my energy to work on the farm. At night, when my parents and everybody went to bed, I'd sneak down the steps to the basement (it was a three-story house) and, very quietly, I'd lift weights. If I heard somebody get up, I'd turn off the lights and play like I wasn't down there. I trained secretively for about two years. Then I got some of my own money, went to a sporting goods store, and ordered a barbell with a 110-pound set of weights. Later on, when I got some more money, I ordered a squat rack, bench press, and a 400-pound Olympic set.

YMCA dues was $15 a year at the time. I joined it and then a health club, which was $48 a year. Prices were cheap back then, but money was very hard for me to come by because I had to work on the farm and my daddy never paid me anything. It's hard to save money when you have no income, so gradually I started doing odd jobs. Then I started ordering vitamin, mineral, and protein supplements to further increase my size, and all of a sudden the kids at school started noticing how big I was and began talking about how big my arms were and all that. It was kind of neat getting all that attention, and the need for attention was a very, very strong motivating force, especially when it came to girls looking at me. That led me into wrestling in high school.

I used to wrestle in the dirt and would challenge two kids at once in school. I was doing judo throws way back then, but I didn't even know what they were; they just came to me naturally. My favorite way of throwing somebody was to grab him on my left side and throw him. It's just a very natural movement for me. I'm right-handed, but my favorite punches became a left ridge hand and a left hook.

On my 18th birthday, I joined the Marines and had my first martial arts lesson in judo during boot camp in 1962. While I was in the Marine Corps, I bulked up to 223 pounds because my dream was to become a professional wrestler. I became that big just by lifting weights seven nights a week. (I took all my barbells with me to the Marine Corps Air Station at Cherry Point, North Carolina, and locked them up.) While I was training, I used to watch aikido and judo guys work out every night at the base gymnasium. In 1963, I started trying some karate classes, but I didn't get into an organized class until the beginning of 1964, when I was stationed on Okinawa.

## THE DOJOS OF OKINAWA

In 1963, I applied to go to Okinawa for one reason and one reason only: I wanted to become a black belt. At first, karate people didn't impress me because most of them were little guys. (Little guys never impressed me with anything.) They had big mouths and were kind of quick, but you could just run them over. I was always a 200-pounder during these years, and I hung around with big 220- 230-pound weight lifters. We always laughed at little guys because you could always just grab them, pick them up, and throw them down—and that was the end of the fight. They could hit you as hard as they wanted, but you didn't feel it. We used to hear these karate guys say things like, "Well, I'll jab you in the eyes," or "I'll kick you in the groin." When you have a 230-pound football player rushing you in a street fight, you can't stand there and calmly pinpoint a finger strike to the eye or deliver an accurate groin kick. Not even black belts can do that.

I recall hearing rumors about a guy named John Korab, about how tough he was. Korab had made his black belt at Cherry Point under a little black belt named Fuji (I guess it was some nickname he got in Japan on Mount Fuji). I went to a couple of their karate classes. They would just stand there with their arms out and make you do 2,000 punches and 2,000 front kicks, and talk about how tough it was. The next night nobody would show up because they were too sore. And every once in a while a black belt would organize a class just to show off how good he was, and nobody would come out the next night.

I wanted to be a black belt, too, and I would watch black belts training in the same gym. On one side of the gym were guys playing basketball. (It was a huge airplane hangar, so it was an incredibly big gym.) On the other side was a judo class, and next to it was a karate class. I would always be over on the far side in the weight room. In between exercises, I'd step into the gym and watch these guys goof off. At the time, I didn't think much of the judo guys because, once in a while, a wrestler would get in there with a judo guy, do a fake, dive at his legs, pick him up, and dunk him down in a fireman's carry or something like that. Also, most of the karate guys were little skinny suckers, so I just couldn't believe in all their hokey moves. Once in a while I'd go over and say, "Hey, show me something!," and these guys would tell me how deadly this move was or how deadly that move was. But there was nothing at all convincing behind what they were doing. I just saw hands and feet waving. It wasn't like a boxing gym where they put gloves on and actually hit each other. I didn't think much of it. In spite of that, I still wanted to be a black belt.

What's interesting is that the day I got to Okinawa, I was put in the same platoon as John Korab. (We were in communications.) Now remember, this is the guy I had heard about. As a matter of fact, the morning after I arrived, he was leading the morning exercises (we had PT or "physical training" at 5:30 every morning). We did a slap-fighting routine for about two minutes, went through about 15 minutes of calisthenics, and at the end of calisthenics we usually jogged or did slap fighting. We would really slap the heck out of each other. Korab wasn't very big—about 164 pounds—but he had huge knuckles, incredibly thick, strong forearms, and a really puffy chest because he did push-ups and punched all the time. You could just tell that he was in incredible shape. He had a thick neck, nice strong jaw, and mean-looking eyes—typical of a black-belt Marine living on Okinawa. (Most of them had those fierce eyes.) Finally, I was impressed. That night I asked some people, "Which is the best karate club to join?" The island was full of karate clubs. They said to go try Eizo Shimabuku, so I went to his class. There was no one there the night I came in and I think it was raining. The year was 1964.

People ask me what I thought of Okinawa back then, but I really didn't care about where I was. All I wanted to do was go to the gym every night and work out. I didn't care about anything else. I never watched TV and I never read the newspaper. I did nothing but train five hours a night, whether it was in the weight room or in the dojo. I was what they call an enthusiastic fanatic.

Korab coincidentally happened to be training and teaching at Shimabuku's dojo, so I kind of lucked out. One day when I was there, a brown belt was being promoted. He was getting ready to go back to the U.S. and he got his black belt. I told him that I was going to lift weights one day and do karate the next. He turned to me and said, "Forget it. You can't lift weights and do karate." It was bad advice, but I took it and, that very day, I quit lifting weights.

Of course, the war in Vietnam was just getting started at the time I was on Okinawa. We were sending advisors in 1963 and '64. My own platoon captain went to Vietnam as an advisor. He got shot in the butt and was captured, so I knew something was going on there, but I didn't even know where Vietnam was. I knew where the gym was and I knew where the dojo was, but I didn't care about the outside world. I was locked into my own little world and lived in my own little mental cage.

My first impression of Mr. Shimabuku was that he was a little bitty guy wearing a red belt and a dark blue gi, not a black gi. He had a bunch of pictures up on his dojo walls and other things such as a Buddha over here and a lion over there, plus kendo sticks, sais, and bos. The dojo was his back yard. There was no ceiling, so when it rained, the water came right down onto the floor. (We would run into his house and wait for the rain to stop, then we'd run right back out.) It had a concrete floor, which is what most of the schools had. Some had dirt floors and others were somebody's back yard. Some of the richer guys had concrete slabs.

In the U.S., most dojos have air conditioning, mats, signs, lights, and such. We had none of that. Class would start mid-evening. I'd get there at about five o'clock, spend an hour on the makiwara board, and then spend another hour side-kicking the heavy bag. Classes started about 7:00 P.M. and the class itself would go for about two hours.

At the base, we would get up at 5:15 A.M., six days a week, fall out at 5:30 A.M., fall in for formation, and then either have an inspection or do physical training for 20 to 30 minutes. At six we'd eat breakfast and about an hour later we'd fall out for formation, a rifle inspection, or something like that. We'd then march to work, which started at 7:30.

I worked in telephone communications and went to Vietnam in 1965 as a member of the first combat unit to go to Vietnam: the 8th Marine Brigade. We were there before the news media knew we were there. I would set up communications between the Navy ships in the harbor and the camps at the base. Sometimes we'd set up communications between the guys out on the front lines and the base at camp, which is called a C.P. (command post). I'd be up on a hill somewhere all by myself, but I only had 20 rounds for each magazine. I'd take two magazines and flip-flop them upside down and tape them together, so as soon as one magazine emptied, I could flip them and put another in. I only had 40 rounds, but the Vietcong never did attack me.

Basically, you could say I was in the service to learn karate. As it turns out, most of the learning was a result of watching others. For example, one day I saw Korab hitting the makiwara and I asked him how long he normally hit it. He said that he worked right hand and left hand, then he'd turn around and do back knuckles. (Some of the guys also would work their forearms.) I'd watch Korab hit the board and then I'd hit it, plus I started doing little things like getting a skin-toughening agent and putting it on my knuckles. I'd grind my knuckles into fine sand, beat them for about 10 minutes, and then continue grinding them into the sand. I'd just pound my fists into the sand. That was the fastest way to build up my knuckles.

Breaking was not important except to the black belts, who would go around and do exhibitions to try to draw new students into their classes. Most classes had up to, but not more than, 20 students. I mentioned that class would begin at 7:00 P.M., but actually it started whenever the sensei wanted to come out and start class. If there were no black belts out there, Shimabuku would teach class himself, but he'd usually come out, bow everybody in, and have Korab or somebody else run the class.

Korab did almost all the teaching, but everybody had a lot of respect for Shimabuku. We would always say "yes, sir" or "no, sir" to him. He spoke pretty good broken English and after a couple of weeks you got used to the accent and could understand what the heck he was saying. I stayed with him for about three and a half months, up until I made green belt. At that time, you could stay on Okinawa as long as you wanted. A Marine's initial tour on "the rock" was for 13 months. (The army and air force guys stayed there for 18 months.) If you were lucky, you could make your black belt in those 13 months. If not, you had to extend your stay for another 12 months or more.

There were a couple of guys who had been there for four years straight. They'd married Okinawans, spoke the language well, and they knew where all the schools were. One of the guys was John Hall. Hall was a short little guy who went to the All Japan Karate Championships in 1964 and took second place. He was the third best black belt in our school and had a very good side kick. John was kind of a nasty little guy; he used to practice rolling around trying to snatch ears off dogs and practicing all kinds of war stuff and throwing sais. The good thing was that he taught me a lot of jujutsu techniques that he had learned on the island.

I loved jujutsu because I loved to grapple. In karate, we were taught some throws and stuff, but they didn't teach a whole lot of choke holds, wrist flexes, takedowns, and comealongs, which is the stuff that I had always liked. John would work me a lot on those jujutsu moves. Meanwhile, I tried hard to find a jujutsu school, but couldn't. The last year I was on Okinawa (1965), I found a really good judo club in Koza City (the guys in this club were much better than the little guys I had first seen practicing judo). I went there after I left Shimabuku's dojo. It's interesting why I left his school.

On Okinawa they have a funny payment schedule. Here in the U.S., when you join a gym and you pay for 30 days, you get 30 days from the day you join. Every month, on the date that you joined, your fee again becomes due. Shimabuku charged $10 the first month and $6 a month after that. I paid him in advance the first day I got there—the 30th of the month. When I handed him the money, I said, "This is for one month." He said, "Yes." Now, when I said one month, I was thinking 30 days. However, according to Okinawan or Japanese time, whether you join on the 30th of the month or not, on the first day of the next month your fee becomes due. So you're basically paying for one day if you join on the 30th. Well, he didn't tell me that. Every month I'd pay Shimabuku on the 20th or 21st, not knowing that I was paying three weeks late, according to his calendar. He started getting uptight for money and one night he came out in front of class and called somebody to pay; the kid went and got the money. Then Shimabuku turned to me and asked, "Joe, you pay?" I said that I had already paid. He got really mad and shouted, "You pay! You pay late every month!" He embarrassed the hell out of me in front of the whole class. It broke my heart. For three months in a row I thought I'd been paying early. (I was trying to impress him. I thought, *I'm going to give him the money a week early. I really like this stuff, so I don't mind paying for it.*) He had told me I could make black belt before I left Okinawa (less than a year), so leaving his dojo at that time would kind of kill my dream, because making black belt was what it was all about. Anyway, I went and got the money to pay him. I was so hurt by what he did that, during kata practice, I took off my green belt, threw it at the front of the school, turned around, and walked off.

Shimabuku was sitting inside and John Hall was in front of the class. Hall asked me what was wrong. I can't remember exactly what my answer was. I just said that I quit and that I wasn't coming back. I walked out the door and never went back. Hall had already told me about another karate school where he'd learned to develop his side kick, so I went there. In fact, I checked out a bunch of schools and ended up going to a little area called Agena Village, which is about 200 yards away from the old Ishinryu school where Tatsu Shimabuku taught. Kinjo Chinsaku became my instructor. The head master, Hohan Soken, eventually tested me for my first-degree black belt, but Kinjo actually gave me the certificate.

When I changed systems, I started all over again as a white belt and was there with Kinjo for three months before I went to the Okinawan Championships, where I was disqualified in the match for first place but took third place. I didn't know what a point was or anything; I just did what they told me to do. When I came back to the dojo, the guys asked how it went and I told them that I had taken third place. I had taken third place with three months of training in brown belt division and was fighting big guys with more than a year of training. The instructor said, "Good." It must have made an impression.

A couple of months later, I noticed something different at the dojo. Up on the wall were everybody's names in Japanese on a wooden plaque. When you were promoted, your name went up there. Gunnery Sergeant Edwards was a second-degree black belt in tang soo do at the dojo. He had started over again as a white belt the same day I had, but he was a black belt in Korea. He could throw high Korean kicks, which Okinawans didn't throw well, and he and I would spar every night. In 1964, at the International Karate Championships, he had fought Mike Stone, so he had been around and took sparring seriously. I knew that he knew what the best was. He was the first person to ever tell me that I was going to be a champ. He said, "I'm not just saying champion. You're going to be a *great* champion—maybe the best!" What he told me I tended to remember, and I began to think that he might be right. I didn't know who Mike Stone was, so the name didn't mean anything to me. However, later on I found out that Mike Stone was beating up everybody in the U.S. Later I realized that Gunny Edwards was already putting me at that level.

## EARNING THE BLACK BELT

I walked into the school one day and there was Gunny Edwards, smiling. Every night when I'd come in, I'd look up on the board to see if I had moved up in rank. There were 10 levels to go through to make black belt and I was moving along pretty quickly. That day, when I entered the dojo, I saw my name up there as a black belt, even though I didn't recall being tested. Then Gunny Edwards walked over and told me, "They're going to make us black belts tonight."

I said, "What? Really? Wow!"

"Remember that old man who came down here and sat in front of the class the other night a couple weeks back?" he asked.

I said, "Yeah, I remember."

"Well, he was a 10th-degree black belt from Naha and he was here to test us that night. That was a test they put us through."

They had put us through the test without telling us. Of course, Kinjo couldn't speak English anyway, so maybe that's why he didn't tell us. He had a fifth-degree Okinawan who spoke broken English who ran the classes. So we were being tested and didn't even know it. (There was no charge for the test. As a matter of fact, my tuition was only $2 a month. Kinjo owned a bus company and a taxi company, so didn't need the money; he taught us for free. The $2 a month he gave to the Naha headquarters. This all took place in December of 1964.)

Here's how it happened. About a week before they gave me the black belt, they put a big pack of rice up in front of the class. They just packed this rice down and it sat there. Every night when I'd come, I'd wonder why the rice was up there. The flies would be on it—all kinds of bugs and such. The night we got promoted, everybody lined up. We had to step up in front of the class and the instructor handed us our new belts. We took our old belts off, put the new belts on, and then took a sip of saki. Then the staff came around and gave everybody a piece of the rice, which we had to eat. After that, the sensei hit each of us on the back with a big kendo stick. Now, in America, they hit you on the arm or in the stomach when you get promoted. Well, they hit you on the back with a stick over there. (The teacher liked that kendo stick. When we would do drills in class, he'd walk around with the stick all during class and knock the hell out of us.)

The day I put on that black belt was the biggest day of my whole life. Making black belt was more important to me than winning any hall of fame award, being written up in *Ring* magazine, being on the cover of a martial arts magazine, or winning the World Championship. There was nothing more important than winning the black belt and nothing ever came close to it. It was all I wanted.

After the promotion, class went on as usual. I continued in Kinjo's school until I was sent to Vietnam, which was about four months later. In Vietnam I taught hand-to-hand combat to Recon. Because the guys there were fighting for real, I didn't teach punches from the hip. I only taught sparring and street combat. My feeling was—and still is—to get in there, get the man on the ground, and choke him out. These guys were on the front line every day. I couldn't afford to make any mistakes.

Few people can say that they have taught hand-to-hand combat to Force Recon in Vietnam. Force Recon is like the Navy's UDTs (Underwater Demolition Teams; the toughest people in all the Navy) and the Army's Rangers. (It was the Rangers who scaled the cliffs at Normandy.) I learned to teach only what works in Vietnam because lives depended on it.

I put in for an extension to stay an extra six months in Vietnam because I liked it. I loved the war zone, plus I got extra pay (what they call hazardous duty or combat pay). I was so at home that I even put up my little makiwara board.

The Marines didn't extend my time in Vietnam because my orders were lost, so they sent me back to Okinawa for my last six months. That provided me with quite an opportunity. All the Marines on Okinawa already had taken off for Vietnam by then (the summer of 1965), so I was elated. I was set up on a radio relay communication set and all I had to do was operate the radios all day long. A couple of other guys and I would take turns. We could relax or work out on the job; anything we wanted. I was my own boss, had two guys under me, and nobody to bother me.

During this time I would go down the island and take lessons from Seiyu Oyata at noon each day. I'd usually get a private lesson from him because at this time of day no one would be there for class. At 6:00 P.M. I'd go to judo class and at 9:00 P.M. I'd go back to Kinjo Chinsaku.

By this time, Shimabuku had heard about my reputation on Okinawa. At one time, I teamed up with a big, strong guy who was in the army. We used to go from dojo to dojo every night, just beating the hell out of any black belt we could get our hands on. All I wanted to do was be a good black belt. I didn't care about anything else. As a matter of fact, I eventually made black belt in three separate styles, but my original certificates were stolen from me, as well as my original gi and my original black belt. Fortunately, before this happened I had given Bill Wallace (world champion and a close friend) some of my competition gis. I understand he's got them still.

Night and day, all I did was work out, practicing karate, weapons, and fighting. When I was on radio watch I'd work all my weapons. That's when I perfected them. My favorites were a hand-made set of sais. They were heavy and really developed my wrists and forearms. I'd spin the nunchuks and work on all the nunchuku tricks. I'd work the sais, kamas, short bo, and long bo. I also spent a lot of time perfecting my side kick with Kinjo.

There is a story about Kinjo that I should tell. The story goes that, when he was a kid, American servicemen killed his parents, so he didn't really like Americans. He had been jumped one time by five men and he killed one of them. Two others were hospitalized and two got away. All he used was the side kick. The authorities put him in prison. Some people he knew petitioned the government and got him out. Naturally, when he taught the side kick, people listened. I really believed in his side kick, but John Hall also had taught me a side kick, and Korab had a dangerous one, too.

John Korab is the one who first taught me how to fight with contact. He had boxed in trade school in the United States, so he held his hands up like a boxer, not down low like a karate man. He really stressed defense and didn't care how many points you scored; all he was concerned with was whether you blocked or not. He taught me defense, too. After a few thousand repetitions a day, I developed lightning speed on my side kick.

I continued to work with Kinjo, too. He would make me perform the switch-over step, touch step, replacement step, and cross-behind step, all of which are incredibly explosive forms of footwork! That's where my offensive footwork began—the exploding footwork (exploding in, exploding back) that I am known for. For this initial style, I credit both Korab and Kinjo.

## A RETURN TO THE STATES

In 1966, I came back to the U.S. and, once again, I was assigned to the same platoon as John Korab. I had been communicating with Korab from Okinawa, where they had tried to make me a fifth degree, but I turned it down because Korab was only a second degree. (I did, however, eventually accept third degree before I came back to the United States.)

Shimabuku had tried to make me a second degree in 1965, but I turned him down, too. I was teaching class outside of camp the day his staff came up to give me the second-degree certificate. Two Okinawan black belts walked in to give me the promotion and one said, "Joe, Shimabuku said you never paid him." Once again, the money thing had come up. "You never paid him for your green and brown belt certificates."

I said, "Wait a minute. First of all, I never got a green belt certificate from the guy. Second, I did pay him, and third, you take this black belt certificate and tell him I don't want it."

They couldn't believe it and walked out. Someone said, "Wow! I never saw anyone turn down a second-degree black belt!"

I said, "You just saw it."

I turned down a lot of rank that a lot of guys only dreamed of having. Korab had turned down a third degree when he left, accepting only a second, and I would have felt guilty for passing him up under the same instructor. A lot of people wanted rank, but Korab and I just didn't see any point to it. From that day on, we had the attitude of, *hey, if you've got a black belt on, then there's nothing higher.* That was the way we saw it.

I was assigned Camp Lejeune, North Carolina, when I returned to the United States in 1966. Korab and I worked out hard together. We ran off most of the other black belts and didn't have any equipment—no bags to side kick. (All of that was left behind.)

We didn't fool around with weapons anymore. Instead, every night we'd choose three katas and do each two or three times at the end of the workout. I never really believed in the value of kata for self-defense. On Okinawa, they work your mind to control things and get you to do it their way. They want you to believe that what they say is the law. The traditional karateka is taught to be good at kata. What they don't realize is that traditional karate is fighting; fighting was here first and they created the kata from the fighting techniques. A lot of people think of it the other way around. Believe me, combat has been here a lot longer than kata or karate.

Anyway, every night I'd work with Korab. It was freezing because it was late January or early February, and we'd go outside in a gi and get really sweaty. We worked out on a sidewalk right outside the gymnasium. Guys would walk by and stare, but no one would ever make a nasty comment toward us. Once in a while somebody would want to work out with us, so we'd bring him over and, half way through the workout, he'd quit and never show up again. Korab would just work anybody into the ground.

The first time I sparred Korab as a black belt, he got a couple of points on me, but after that (about May of 1966) I was pretty hard to hit. We would spar for 30 minutes non-stop at the end of every one of our workouts. At the end, when your muscles are tired, you can tell what mistakes you're making. At that point in time, in my mind he was by far the best black-belt fighter in the entire world. I don't think anybody could come close to touching him. Once in a while I'd score a point on him, and once in a while he'd score a point on me, but most of the time we'd spar for 30 minutes straight and neither of us would score a point. Again, the emphasis was on defense, defense, defense, and we would explode back and forth—Pow! Pow! Pow!

The 1966 Nationals were written up in the Camp Lejeune newspaper and Korab was talking about it. He had heard about a guy named Thomas LaPuppet, who had won the Camp Lejeune tournament, and who had also won Henry Cho's All-American Karate Championships. LaPuppet was a very big name. In fact, in his very first match he had beaten Tony Tulleners, who had won Ed Parker's California State Championships, and had fought Mike Stone in the finals at the Internationals. In 1966, Tony won an all-expense-paid trip to Jhoon Rhee's U.S. National Championships. I fought LaPuppet that night in the finals and zapped him two to nothing. That day, Tony Tulleners was the best competitor on the West Coast and Thomas LaPuppet was the best competitor on the East Coast. It's safe to say that the competition was pretty stiff. I had only 22 months of training under my belt, so I did pretty well; only one point was scored against me during the entire tournament.

Korab didn't think much of tournament guys. He'd sit and watch the tournaments, but his attitude was pretty much, why bother? He wouldn't enter tournaments because, like Bruce Lee, he didn't think tournaments meant anything. After all, they were not making contact. On Okinawa, when we did our serious sparring, we wore kendo gear—the wire mask, gloves, fiberglass chest protector, and cup—and we'd kick and punch for real. When we came back to the United States, punches were being pulled. We just thought it was hokey. The purpose of a punch or kick is to do damage. If you don't make contact, how can you measure the effectiveness of a technique?

I wanted to make the kata championships, too. I won first place black belt in kata, first place in black belt sparring, and the Grand Championship in my first tournament. My form was sanchin, with my shirt off. I was very muscular, had a nice tan, and I did it like it was never done before. By the next year, I had several fans who would come up and congratulate me after each win. One guy gave me a check for $100.

During that first year, I won the Chicago version of the World Karate Championships and also the Northwest Karate Championships in Tacoma, Washington. But when I had competed in the 1966 U.S. National Championships, I was still in the Marine Corps. I knew nothing about how to enter a tournament, compete, or play the politics. When I went to the 1966 National Championships, I had just planned to sit and watch. I'd never seen a tournament before.

I walked into Jhoon Rhee's school the night before the tournament because they had a meeting and, of course, when I got there, I got there early. No one else was there. Jhoon Rhee and another Korean guy took me into the office and questionned why I wasn't competing.

I said, "No, I just came up here to watch."

They talked me into competing, got my five bucks and my application, and told me to show up at nine the next morning.

I was there at nine o'clock the next morning, sitting in a gi, warmed up, ready to go. I didn't know anything about tournaments, so I thought, *Gee, we're gonna fight right now*. At 5:30 that afternoon I had my first match. I ended up sitting in a chair for eight long hours waiting for that fight.

I didn't referee because I didn't know anything about how to call a point. Nobody knew my name; I just sat there. I would have kept sitting there, but eventually someone did call my name and by then I was ready to fight. In my first four matches I ripped four gis off. I just grabbed the gis and ripped them off as I punched. (I used the overhead punch.) Sometimes I'd grab a gi, pull the arm up, and side kick underneath. I only had two quick movements—grab, pull them off balance, and punch; and grab, then side kick. It worked because the guys weren't used to the power and I could get them really fast.

### TRAINING WITH BRUCE LEE

When I left the Marine Corps, I went straight to Hollywood because I wanted to get into films to make some money. I opened a school with Bob Wall in 1967, but I didn't like running a karate school, so in '68 I sold the school to Chuck Norris. (When I opened my school, I could only work with white belts. They had to be taught and I was the teacher. When you spar with white belts for six months and avoid the competition, you lose the edge. I lost my desire.)

Fortunately, someone came along who gave me the inspiration and desire to start moving forward again. I met Bruce Lee in 1967, and in '68 Mike Stone convinced me to start working with Bruce. I didn't think much of Bruce at first because his art was kung fu and he was very small, but my opinion of him soon changed. I worked hard with him and won 11 tournaments in a row, non-stop. Bruce asked me to tell people that I was studying jeet kune do and that I was working under him, which I did. In fact, I had him stand beside me at one of Rhee's U.S. National Championships as my instructor when I received the trophy. I could tell that he liked that. I was the defending champion, he was a special guest, and he ended up as instructor to the grand champion.

I liked jeet kune do because Bruce got me into doing more movement with my head. Because I'm right handed, he took me back to my right side forward, which I was using on Okinawa. (I had temporarily switched over to my left side because, in my first National Championships, I had hurt my right heel. When I fought in the National Championships, I put my left side forward because I could use either side. I still won the tournament, even with my left side forward.) Bruce switched me back right side, or what in JKD is called strong side forward. He got me to use more release on the end of my kicks and punches, rather than tightening up at the end (I could then release my power and have more follow through). Bruce taught me to block with the rear hand instead of the front hand. He re-emphasized explosiveness, which I already had. He was the perfect coach for me.

Eventually, I went through his whole system. We practiced single-hand sticking hand, energy drills, Bruce's style of vertical punching, trapping, and one-inch punching. At first I was signed up for private lessons, but eventually I would just show up without any set time. A lot of time was spent talking, exchanging philosophy, watching fight films, and such. Bruce and I never actually put on gear to spar, but we would do the JKD drills he was trying to develop. All the time I worked with Bruce—over a year or two—we never worked at his school. We met at his home, at a restaurant, or at a tournament. He was a very charming guy.

I used to practice all the time with my own sparring partners. When I would go to parties, we would end up doing some of Bruce's drills, like sticking hands. We would just touch wrists (or engage and clear an obstruction, as it was called) and try to see who could touch and get one hand in the better position. That's how I developed a lot of speed. I'd work with guys who weighed 140 pounds. Using what Bruce had shown me, I learned to beat to the punch even the little lightning-fast black belts. Eventually, I think it was about 1969, I quit training with Bruce, but I kept practicing and started teaching JKD principles in karate seminars across the country. I always told people where the technique came from when I taught a JKD technique and I would give credit to Bruce. The karate guys didn't care where it came from, so long as it worked.

The sticking hands, among other things, were also used in karate. I used to go down to the goju schools on Okinawa where they all did the sticking-hands technique. In goju, they did one-side sticking hands, whereas the wing chun guys would do both-sides sticking hands. About this time (1968), I started going to a boxing gym. (Bruce admired boxing because boxers hit for real.) People would hear about me, come down to my karate schools, and tell me I should get into boxing, because they just love that tenacious way I had of just attacking straight ahead. I had a sort of relentless pressure and aggressiveness about me. A group of people who were working with Sugar Ray Robinson saw this and they sent me down to the Main Street Boxing Gym so that Sugar Ray could train me. I went down there to work with Sugar Ray a couple of times, but some other guys kind of stole me away from him and began to teach me. I started going down to the gym every day and bought gloves, hand wraps, and all that stuff.

Then, in the latter part of 1968, I fought in a Chuck Norris tournament—a Pro-Am thing—and Joe Orbilo was in the audience. Joey was ranked number five in the world heavyweight division in 1965-66 by *Ring* magazine. He and I started working together and he began teaching me how to box. He gradually shifted me from the right-side-forward stance that Bruce had made me use, back to left-side forward, and I started going down to the Sea Side Gym, a boxing gym in Long Beach. I'd meet Joe there every day at about three in the afternoon, before all the pros came in. That's when I put the boxing into kicking and started kickboxing.

## THE BIRTH OF AMERICAN KICKBOXING AND FULL-CONTACT KARATE

In 1969, one of my students, Lee Faulkner (who was a stunt man and a production man in the film industry), wanted to promote karate. To do so, he created a world championship East Coast-West Coast-Midwest team competition. Mike Stone, Chuck Norris, Skipper Mullins, Bob Wall, and I represented the West Coast. (Bob was put on the team by the promoter.) Before the event, I told Lee that I was not going to fight in point tournaments anymore. I was sick and tired of them. I had won the National Championships, the International Championships, and the World Karate Championships, and I figured that I had won it all. I was a black belt and no one could beat me, but I was tired of these little bitty wimps jumping in there and touching me with their hands or their feet, and then running away from me for the next two minutes thinking, *yeah, I beat the champion, Joe Lewis*. So from then on it was going to be full contact.

I knew these karate guys couldn't last more than 30 seconds in full contact. I'd go down to the gym and spar some of Chuck Norris' black belts. Chuck was one of the best teachers and fighters ever, and he turned out very good black belts. I put the boxing gloves on the black belts and they started throwing kicks. I'd step inside, jam or smother the kicks, catch them with a left hook, and knock them right down. It seemed too easy at the time.

▼

From wrestling and weight lifting as a teen to mastering a rough-and-tumble contact version of Okinawan karate, Joe Lewis seemed destined for greatness. The U.S. National Championships of

1966, a tournament of prestige with a title created by America's finest karate fighters, seemed all too easy a win to the youthful, athletically gifted Lewis. In a few short years he had won it all and had become discouraged with the simplicity of his task. As fate would have it, he met the legendary Bruce Lee, perhaps the most successful martial artist of all time. Lee reintroduced Lewis to the strategy of the fight. With Lee as his mentor, Lewis became unbeatable and, once again, grew discouraged with the ease of which he could win.

A chance meeting with world heavyweight boxing contender Joey Orbilo reignited Lewis' interest in contact fighting. In point fighting he become king of the hill. Even Bill "Superfoot" Wallace, three-time national champion, said of Lewis, "I might out-point him in the tournament ring, but everyone knows who could win in a real fight."

Boxing training brought a taste of reality to Lewis. In 1970, he fought the first full-contact karate/kickboxing match in the United States (in California). Employing the right-hand method of jeet kune do, Lewis knocked out the California heavyweight champion, Greg Baines, in the second round. In almost a dozen fights to follow, Lewis knocked out every opponent.

With a record of no losses, Lewis entered the World Championship for full-contact karate to represent the U.S. as a heavyweight fighter. To no one's surprise, Lewis knocked out his European opponent in the first round. The legend of Joe Lewis had been fully established. A decade later, he was voted "The Greatest Karate Fighter of All Time" by *Karate Illustrated*. (The leading sport magazine of the day, *Karate Illustrated* polled many of America's top black belts, including Chuck Norris and Mike Stone, who had both scored among the top five.)

Lewis began studying for an acting career in 1970. He starred in five action-adventure films, including *Jaguar Lives*, *Force Five*, *The Cutoff*, and *Death Cage*. He also appeared in several television series and made guest appearances on numerous talk shows, including those of Joey Bishop, Johnny Carson, Dinah Shore, and Merv Griffin.

Since 1984, Lewis has turned his talents and energies toward a professional teaching career. Again, he has been highly successful in this field. In 1987, for example, he taught 140 seminars in 80 cities in eight countries, in addition to making personal appearances at tournaments and other martial arts functions and charity benefits.

Lewis' research has led to the production of more than 25 one-of-a-kind instructional videos. He remains active, playing characters in films and writing for several martial arts publications worldwide. An article he wrote concerning self-defense for older Americans appeared in the January 29, 1995, issue of *Parade*, and in the June 30, 1996, issue of *Parade* he authored an article highlighting the importance of martial arts instruction for kids.

Lewis recently won two North Carolina Governor's Awards for his efforts in crime prevention. He is the only fighter to have won the World Championships as both an amateur and a professional, the U.S. National Championships four times, the Internationals three times, and is one of only two men (the other being Mike Stone) to win all three. Lewis is one of only two men to have held both the World Karate Championships and the World Kickboxing Championships titles at the same time.

His other accomplishments are many. The following synopsis of records set and innovations further attests to the extent of Joe Lewis' contributions to American martial arts:

• In 1966, Lewis won the first official American karate tournament, the U.S. Nationals, entering without having seen or previously participated in such an event, and became the amateur world karate champion (point fighting).

• In 1967, Lewis became the first karate competitor to ever appear on the cover of any national martial arts magazine. Prior to this, competitors never had been allowed to appear on the covers. (Only heads of organizations or martial arts systems, primarily Asian, were considered cover material.) Lewis spearheaded putting the sport of karate and kickboxing on national television. In 1967, he created a top-ten ratings list for American karate fighters.

• In 1968, Lewis became the first professional heavyweight karate champion (point fighting). Also in 1968, he became the first of Bruce Lee's students to teach jeet kune do principles to a national audience.

• In 1970, Lewis became the first fighter to do kickboxing in America, knocking out Greg Baines in the second round. (Baines was the California State Heavyweight Champion and International Heavyweight Karate Champion.) Lewis was the one who converted the sport of karate into a full-contact sport, known today as kickboxing.

• Between 1969 and 1971, Lewis became a three-time winner of the Internationals.

• In 1971, he became the U.S. Heavyweight Kickboxing Champion (full contact) and was featured in *Sports Illustrated* and *The Ring*.

• In 1973, he co-hosted a national talk show completely devoted to the martial arts (Merv Griffin). Also in 1973, he created a revolutionary scientific approach to fighting, which he subsequently taught to many American karate champions.

• In 1974, Lewis obtained international television coverage of the sport of karate for the first time in nine years. The sport had been blacklisted from national television since 1965, when ABC aired the bloody finals of the televised National Championships. He also launched kickboxing as a televised sport in 1974, along with his student, Tom Tannenbaum, then senior vice president at Universal Television. The 90-minute special aired on ABC's *Wide World of Entertainment*.

• In 1976, Lewis was voted "The Greatest Fighter of All Time" in *Karate*, a French publication. This publication was distributed in more than 25 countries and had the largest circulation in the world at that time.

• In 1983, Lewis was voted the "Top Karate Player of All Time" in an international survey conducted by Rainbow Publications, *Black Belt,* and *Karate Illustrated*. Lewis was the only fighter voted to the top-ten list by everyone polled.

• In 1988, Lewis, along with partners Bill Wallace and Jerry Beasley, developed the now world-famous Karate College martial arts summer camp at Radford University in Radford, Virginia.

Each year, several hundred students are introduced to this intense three-day study of fighting systems from around the world.

 • At one time, in addition to having been inducted into 11 halls of fame, Lewis was the only karate competitor to have ever been featured in *Ring*, *Gentleman's Quarterly*, and *Sports Illustrated*. Not only was he the first in his sport ever to be featured in those publications, but he also was the first in his sport to be featured in muscle magazines, such as *Strength and Health* (1967).

 • In 1994, at the youthful age of 50, Joe Lewis was recognized for a lifetime of accomplishments and was granted the rank of 10th-degree black belt.

 In the next chapter, we will examine some of the skills and strategies of the Joe Lewis American Karate Systems.

# CHAPTER TWO

# Joe Lewis on Theory and Practice in the Joe Lewis American Karate Systems

I believe that what Bruce Lee meant when he said that a good puncher would beat a good kicker any day was that the closer you get to your opponent, the better your accuracy, and that's important. That means that at grappling range you have more accuracy than at punching range, and at punching range you have more accuracy than at kicking range. (That doesn't mean that if someone has only kicked all of his life that he should have better accuracy with his punches, or that he should have better accuracy with his grappling.)

In a real situation, I prefer to get in close and get my opponent on the ground. I like to fight on the ground. That's my style. The Brazilian jujutsu fighters are pretty much the same way. They like to get in behind you, get you on the ground, and choke you out. Well, for years, that's been my basic premise. However, you have to keep in mind that your style depends on different factors, such as your physical makeup—how you are built—in conjunction with your psychological nature. For instance, some people are very trigger happy. They like to drive up on the firing line; they have a strong appetite to get in there and get it over with right away. That's the way I am and I've been like that since I was a child. Some people are laid back and like to play more of a waiting game; they're a little more passive. Such people tend to be more of what we call the striker types. In any case, you've got to know yourself and understand whether you favor inside fighting or outside fighting. But even though I'm more of an inside fighter, my systems are not necessarily designed strictly for those who like to fight on the inside.

When I'm out there actually sparring or fighting, I take those two factors which determine my style and I tie in one other factor: focus. When I'm focusing, I always put my attention on my opponent. My reaction is based on what my opponent does and depends on what my eyes see in conjunction with what my basic strategy dictates.

Since the law of strategy says that you have to control your opponent in any given situation, I have to be able to control my opponent in any zone, whether I'm on the inside or outside, or in the medium zone. This is what the Joe Lewis systems are about—to help you become a balanced fighter and teach you how to adjust to any opponent in any situation. For example, if you're up against a good kicker on the outside, you're going to be playing in and out of his trap. Don't get caught between the knee and the foot, because that's where a good kicker wants you. I would play him inside the knee and outside the foot to stay off his line of fire. I would keep circling him, using lateral motion, feinting left, feinting right, and try to deny him access to the target on the outside zone. Therefore, on the outside and inside I would have a strong offense. But against a wrestler who likes to fight on the inside, I might completely reverse this strategy.

There's always an absence of space in the case of grappling, and a presence of space in the case of kicking and punching. The amount of space that exists between two opponents determines what zone they're in. At kicking range, techniques such as the long-range kick or the straight-leg kick (in which the leg is only slightly bent) are executed in what we call the outside zone. In the medium zone, we have the short-range kicks, like a spin back kick or a defensive side kick, in which the knee is bent when contact is made. You can almost fire knees at medium distance. You execute your sweeps at medium distance and you work your long-range punches (in which the elbow is basically straight) at medium distance. Then, as you come in closer to what some people call the trapping zone (the paralyzing zone), you can mix the trapping zone in together with the inside zone, or grappling zone. In this zone, you can do takedowns, short-range punches (in which the elbows are bent, as in the short uppercut), short hooks, short body shots, elbow strikes, grabs, head butts, knees, sweeps, shin kicks, heels to the back of the opponent's leg, bites, head locks, comealongs, and wrist flexes. Some people also like to break this zone down into mat work, as opposed to stand-up grappling. Of course, all mat work takes place on the inside, so I like to refer to the inside zone as generally those areas standing up in close and everything that takes place on the ground.

Again, my systems are designed to make you a balanced fighter. What I mean by balanced is not necessarily that you're just as good a puncher as you are a kicker, but that you're equally skilled defensively and offensively in all three zones.

Let me explain this from a strategic point of view, which might be a little too advanced for some beginners. (I have to point you in the right direction here and now, because although all black belts should be teaching this, many aren't.)

When you begin a match or a real altercation, your game plan—your strategy—has to have balance in the form of a defensive side and an offensive side. Let me first explain the defensive side, because your game plan should always be structured from the premise of defense first, offense second. The idea is that, when you step into the ring, you don't want to get hit or hurt. For example, if I'm up against a good outside fighter, what I'm going to do on the outside is to set up a good, strong defense. I don't want to get hit out there, so I'm going to make sure that I keep my hands up in front of my body and face. I'm going to stay off of his line of fire. I'm also going to stay in perpetual motion by moving parts of my body, my position, and my fire power in an attempt to deny him access to the target. So that's the key: the defensive, long-term game plan, which you're going to use all the way through the match, involves denying access to the target so that you don't get hit. By your moving all the time, he's not going to be able to get out there and throw fast, fancy kicks at you or get on the inside with a quick hand combination. You're going to make him hesitate before he fires.

Conversely, we have what is called the short-term strategy, which involves individual setups that you're going to use from one offensive movement pattern to the next. These are short-term offensive game plans that you use because you can't beat somebody with only a defensive strategy. Sooner or later, you've got to get out there, approach the man, and hit him. So to make this approach easier, it's best that you try to use some sort of a setup to get access to the target. In each one of these movement patterns you want to set up your opponent. The patterns are all interconnected and interwoven with your overall long-term strategy. The defensive and offensive frames of mind coexist like the yin and yang balance in the martial arts, and most people do not go out there with a defensive game plan. They only have some idea in mind offensively, but they forget about or overlook the idea that what makes your offense strong is to always be firing and offensively attacking your opponent from a defensively strong position.

▼

According to Lewis, "We should learn the simple things first, and then get into the more advanced, so that, ultimately, we can come back to the basics and perfect them. The secret of being a master is to perfect the basics." Lewis often tells his audience about how he learned the basics on Okinawa and how he spent hundreds of hours perfecting each individual movement. In this section, we introduce the reader to the fundamental stances, kicks, and punches used in the Joe Lewis American Karate Systems. Rest assured that a photo can never adequately convey the power, speed, and self-assurance demonstrated by a master performer such as Lewis.

FIGURE 1

FIGURE 2

## BASIC SKILLS

Defensive blocking has been adapted to the Joe Lewis American Karate Systems to favor mobility. In figures 1 and 2, Lewis demonstrates the traditional low block with the head fully exposed and hand held low next to the hip. This represents a defensively poor decision for self-defense.

In figure 3, Lewis demonstrates the JLAKS-style low block with the body protected and the reverse hand held in a counterattack position. The middle block (figure 4) and the high block (figure 5) are demonstrated in sequence, followed by a reverse mid block (figure 6) and an outside block (figure 7), with a return to a neutral, on-guard position (figure 8).

FIGURE 3

FIGURE 4

FIGURE 5

FIGURE 6

FIGURE 7

FIGURE 8

In the next sequence, Lewis demonstrates the jab, or straight lead hand, and the back fist. From an on-guard position (figure 9), Lewis demonstrates the basic jab (figure 10) and a variation known as the vertical fist (figure 11). Again from an on-guard position (figure 12), Lewis begins the back fist (figures 13–15). It is important to allow the hand to move first to avoid telegraphing the technique.

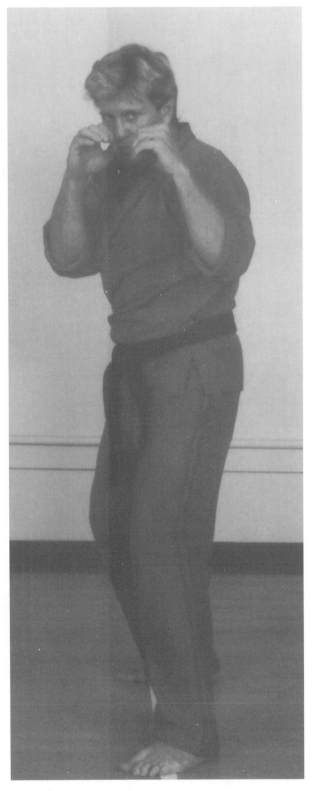

FIGURE 9

FIGURE 10

FIGURE 11

FIGURE 12

FIGURE 13

FIGURE 14

FIGURE 15

FIGURE 16

FIGURE 17

FIGURE 18

FIGURE 19

FIGURE 20

FIGURE 21

FIGURE 22                    FIGURE 23                    FIGURE 24

In the sequence at left, Lewis demonstrates the hook, ridge hand, and reverse punch (or cross). From the on-guard position (figure 16), Lewis shifts his weight forward as if initiating a lead-hand strike (figure 17), then sets up the hook by shifting his weight back to the reverse side (figure 18). The ridge hand is performed in the same manner (figure 19). Returning to the on-guard position (figure 20), Lewis sets up the reverse punch (figure 21).

In sequence 22–24, Lewis demonstrates the basic upper cut punch. Note that the striking fist travels a short distance (from the chest to the head). Power is gained by lifting the hips.

Putting the techniques together, Lewis demonstrates the lead-hand potential with the hook (figures 25–26), followed by the ridge hand (figures 27–29), and the upper cut (figures 30–32). The student must perform many repetitions to gain control of the lead hand.

FIGURE 25

FIGURE 26

FIGURE 27

FIGURE 28

FIGURE 29

FIGURE 30

FIGURE 31

FIGURE 32

By working with a partner, the lead-hand jab can be combined with the parry or block. In this sequence (figure 33), Lewis initiates a jab (figure 34) and then prepares for his partner to jab (figures 35–36). Lewis is careful to parry or stop the jab (figure 37) before contact. The same type of parry can be adapted to stop the front kick or lead-leg straight kick (figures 38–39).

FIGURE 33

FIGURE 34

FIGURE 35

FIGURE 36

FIGURE 37

FIGURE 38

FIGURE 39

FIGURE 40

FIGURE 41

FIGURE 42

FIGURE 43

FIGURE 44

An excellent basic combination to work on and perfect is demonstrated in this sequence and includes the lead jab (figures 40-41), lead (front) kick (figure 42), and reverse punch (figure 43).

The major characteristic of the JLAKS style is mobility. Here, Lewis introduces a basic drill. To move left, move the left foot first (figures 44-45). To move right, move the right foot first (figure 46).

FIGURE 45

FIGURE 46

FIGURE 47

FIGURE 48

FIGURE 49

FIGURE 50

FIGURE 51

FIGURE 52

FIGURE 53

FIGURE 54

FIGURE 55

In this sequence, Lewis demonstrates footwork patterns including the ready position (figure 47), on guard (figure 48), step left (figure 49), reposition (figure 50), step back (moving the back foot first; figure 51), reposition (figure 52), move left (figure 53), reposition (figure 54), and advance forward (moving the front foot first; figure 55). This sequence is often performed at high speed in both left and right lead.

FIGURE 56

FIGURE 57

FIGURE 58

FIGURE 59

At age 39, Lewis demonstrates the power of his fists at a kickboxing event in Charlotte, North Carolina. He prepares (figure 56) to quickly assault his opponent (figures 57-58). Seconds later, the fight ends in a knockout (figure 59). It was speedy knockouts like this one that led to Lewis' title of "Greatest Karate Fighter of All Time."

Sometimes referred to as shadow sparring or shadow boxing, Lewis demonstrates a series of footwork drills that combine fakes with strikes. He begins with a fake low (figures 60–61), repositions (figure 62), then advances forward with a fake (figure 63), steps left (figure 64), repositions (figure 65), then steps left (figure 66) and quickly shifts right (figure 67). He then follows with a straight lead (figure 68), repositions (figure 69), and follows with a low jab (figure 70) and a front kick (figure 71). Lewis ends the front kick with a jab (figure 72), which occupies the opponent while he chooses to retreat (figure 73) with a jab, reposition (figure 74), and advance with a jab (figure 75), followed by a cross or reverse punch (figure 76) and a front kick (figure 77). Lewis repositions (figure 78) and finishes the sequence with a power side kick (figures 79-80).

One would be tempted to call an extended sequence such as figures 60-80 a kata. However, the skills may be changed to suit the performer.

FIGURE 60

FIGURE 61

FIGURE 62

FIGURE 63

FIGURE 64

FIGURE 65

FIGURE 66

FIGURE 67

FIGURE 68

FIGURE 69

FIGURE 70

FIGURE 71

FIGURE 72

FIGURE 73

FIGURE 74

FIGURE 75

FIGURE 76

FIGURE 77

FIGURE 78

FIGURE 79

FIGURE 80

Next, Lewis demonstrates a focus-pad drill using the front kick (figure 81), chambering the front kick (figure 82), full extension (figure 83), a return to on guard (figure 84), chambering the reverse front kick (figure 85), full extension of the front kick (figure 86), and a return to the on-guard position (figure 87).

FIGURE 81

FIGURE 82

FIGURE 83

FIGURE 84

FIGURE 85

FIGURE 86

FIGURE 87

FIGURE 88

FIGURE 89

FIGURE 90

FIGURE 91

In this sequence, Lewis demonstrates the round kick: on guard (figure 88), chamber (figure 89), and extension to contact (figure 90). By returning to the on-guard position (figure 91), Lewis is now able to work the round kick from the front side: first the chamber (figure 92) and then the extension (figures 93–94).

**45**

FIGURE 92

FIGURE 93

FIGURE 94

FIGURE 95

FIGURE 96

FIGURE 97

FIGURE 98

FIGURE 99

By employing the same stance, Lewis begins practice for the front-leg hook kick: on guard (figure 95), chamber (figure 96), and extension (figures 97–99).

Lewis has his partner change position for the ax kick: on guard (figure 100), chamber (figure 101), and contact (figures 102–103).

FIGURE 100

FIGURE 101

FIGURE 102

FIGURE 103

Here, Lewis demonstrates the spinning side kick: on guard (figure 104), spin (figures 105-106), chamber (figure 107), and contact (figure 108).

FIGURE 104

FIGURE 105

FIGURE 106

FIGURE 107

FIGURE 108

# CHAPTER THREE

# Joe Lewis on Skills: Combinations, the Theory of Attack, and the Limited Value of Kata

## THE FOUR RULES OF COMBINATIONS

**W**henever you set up combinations, there are four basic rules to follow. Rule number one is to make sure you have good, quick lead-off techniques, such as a lead-hand punch, a quick kick (like a jab), or a feint. You must use an extension or probing technique to lead into some kind of destruction, trap, grab, or sweep. Any of these tools can be used to help your lead or deceptive lead-off technique.

The second rule is to make sure that you employ good, quick, explosive penetration and clearing speed. You have to be able to move in and out on your opponent very quickly.

The third rule of the successful combination is to make sure that you use a good power technique. For example, I might begin my attack with a little punch, kick, and another punch, then *bam!* I strike with my power technique. When setting up your combinations, make sure you use your favorite power technique, which can be either a punch or a kick. Try to perfect several combinations that you can use.

The fourth rule of good combinations involves negating any gaps in your offensive rhythm. As soon as you finish penetrating, never pause. A pause is a gap. Make sure that as soon as you finish the attack or penetration that you immediately clear. Get out of the way of a counter by your opponent. Move! This is especially true for the end of your technique. Never stop and never hesitate. Pull out of your opponent's space immediately. Bump your opponent immediately, too. Fire as you pull out, or pull out in a different direction than that in which you entered. This will confuse your opponent and make it more difficult for him to counter. Make sure you observe this basic rule. We sometimes call this closing the door behind you as you disengage to regroup and reload.

Besides good penetration and clearing speed, you need good penetration techniques. With good penetration speed, clearing speed, and penetration techniques, you can work your way in and, using techniques, work your way out. You *must* have penetration techniques and clearing techniques so that you can keep your opponent busy while you're penetrating and clearing.

## THE LIMITED VALUE OF KATA

Traditional karate, to me, was fighting. Katas came later. I found that they were practical for training but got away from fighting applications in terms of what actually works. I go back to traditional karate by bypassing katas altogether because they do not teach footwork, timing, or proper breathing—at least not the way you breathe when you are actually sparring—nor do they teach you how to fake, set up an opponent, or how to mentally and physically prepare or apply principles of movement in relation to an opponent. And katas certainly do not teach you how to be tough and absorb punishment. In short, katas simply do not teach you anything to do with reality fighting. Everything in the kata is based on make-believe scenarios created by one individual's idea of what combat should ideally represent.

To learn how to fight, you must always move in relationship to an opponent—a *real* opponent, not an imaginary opponent. Katas do not teach you the psychological attitude needed to focus. When you are doing a kata, you are internally focused. But when you are sparring, you must be externally focused. You can't be internally focused and pay attention to your opponent. Ask yourself, "What's the most important thing about the opponent that needs attention?" If there is no opponent in front of you, you can't ask that question.

Therefore, realistically, katas can destroy your ability to properly focus. Katas do not allow you to complete your physical preparation so that your body is conditioned for contact. These are two of the most important things in fighting, because fights are won in the gym, not in the ring. In the gym you must master your physical preparation and the execution of your technique. When you put those two things together, then the last thing comes into play: you must have the right mind-set.

The right mind-set allows you to focus. Again, ask yourself, "What is it about the opponent that needs attention?" From there you can choose the right game plan, the right strategy. For example, if I'm going to fight someone who is small and fast, I'm not going to use the same game plan that I would use to fight someone big and slow. I've got to have the right game plan so that I have confidence in myself. This confidence enables me to have the will and the power to execute techniques effectively. I need that courage. In a real fight, this ability comes from two sources: knowledge and courage. Kata does not give you the knowledge or the courage to execute in a realistic situation.

To add to the problem faced by some traditional stylists who focus solely on kata, we need to understand that katas do not teach you how to adjust to different types of opponents. If I'm out there actually sparring—making full contact—I'm able to quickly adjust to any opponent in any given situation. Therefore, you must practice in a manner that closely reflects the problem you need to solve. When most people step into the ring or onto the street, they're thinking about what they're going to do to the opponent, which is incorrect. When you get ready to step into the ring, you must have your preparation already down. You already know subconsciously what you're going to do. You've done it a thousand times before under similar circumstances. The minute you step into the ring, you must be able to put your attention on your opponent and make him fight *your* fight. If you don't get hit, you can't be beaten.

The key is *don't get hit*. You must never allow yourself to be separated from the defensive. The instant you step into the ring, you must win the first contact. Let him know that he's walked into *your* office and *you* are in charge! Become the psychological aggressor and seize the offensive right from the start. You need the right attitude to accomplish this assignment and you're not going to find it in katas. Katas do absolutely nothing to prepare you to become the psychological aggressor. The bottom line is that, if you want to be good at fighting, you've got to fight. Nothing else comes close.

## Mobility

Some people have great punches and great kicks, but lack footwork. Therefore, they lack balance. They can stand still and throw a fast punch or a fast kick, but if they can't move fast, they can't hit consistently. They must bridge the gap and hit the opponent.

You need mobility for several reasons. In order to execute a fast offensive technique, you've got to be able to explode quickly off of the firing line as you punch at your opponent's defensive perimeter. You also need footwork for defensive reasons. In order to deny your opponent access to the target or to make him miss, you've got to be able to move quickly defensively. You need footwork because the only way to deal with opponents who have advantages over you (including advantages in reach, height, or speed) is to have some kind of game plan that will help you negate those advantages.

This concept is the cornerstone of my systems. You must learn how to eliminate the opponent's strengths by breaking his advantages and using his weaknesses to approach from a position of superiority. Superior footwork will allow you to set up your opponent and will make it easier for you to eliminate his advantages.

Let's think on a mechanical level. If you consider the importance of stances, kicks, punches, blocks, and footwork—all the mechanics of my systems, or any system—in my opinion, footwork is by far the most important. My systems vary considerably from traditional karate in that they are actually designed around the principles of self-defense, as opposed to offense. The best defense is a good offense; however, schools that teach offensive karate fail to understand two basic principles of a strong offense: 1) a strong offense is one which keeps your opponent busy at all times. This means that whenever you get near your opponent's firing line or just inside his defensive perimeter (where he can hit you), you must at all times be firing the instant you get to his firing line or inside of it, and 2) you better be moving. Those are the only two things you can use when fighting with my systems, or any system, which will enable you to keep him occupied so he can't fire at you. That's what I mean by a strong offense.

A strong offense has no gaps in it. Many fighters step in to hit an opponent with a punch or a combination, strike one or two times, and then stop! They are pausing inside the opponent's firing line. At that point they are unable to keep the opponent busy. (You often see this gap in point fighting.) Traditional drills taught in karate schools go punch, punch, kick, stop! Another is you throw a punch, reposition, then throw a kick; there's a little gap between the punch and the kick. In my system, as your hand is going back, the knee is going out for the kick. Here, then, is the difference between traditional karate and the JLAKS.

Two other problems with traditional karate are that there is too much weight on the rear foot and the feet are too far apart. (You don't want your stance too narrow, either.) Your stance should emphasize mobility and balance at the same time. In JLAKS, moving toward your opponent is called *penetration*. Pulling away from your opponent is called *clearing*. When inside your opponent's defensive perimeter, you *must* keep him busy—keep firing and keep him moving! This concept isn't a part of traditional karate, either, in which practitioners fire the various techniques and, on the last technique, stop (they walk back and get ready for the next technique). By doing this they are unknowingly teaching themselves to put a gap in their defense—they kind of pause as if admiring their work or as if they are waiting for someone to take their picture—and that's when they get hit.

The traditional form of karate has divorced itself from the real fight, in which you must hit and then reposition to avoid being hit. The new karate is derived from the make-believe kata in which no one hits back. We have to get back to the original purpose of karate—to win the fight—and that requires an emphasis on mobility, penetration, and clearing.

## Perfecting the Basics

In terms of personal protection, you must have as a priority defense and conditioning, and then go to punching, kicking, and grappling. I believe you should learn the simple things first and then get into the more advanced, so that ultimately you can come back to the basics and perfect them. The secret of being a master is being able to perfect the basics. But remember, attitude is first and defense is second. Your attitude must be that you will never surrender, never throw in the towel, never give up, never quit, and never yield your position. You can't beat someone who will never quit.

Americans deserve the credit for taking Oriental systems and introducing the modern concept of sport karate. You will notice that throughout the world American fighters are recognized for their innovation in fighting systems. In the Joe Lewis systems, we employ boxing-type hand routines in conjunction with fencing principles, which emphasize the lead-hand techniques. In other words, you want the weapon (the hand or foot) to move first. For instance, my favorite kick is the lead-leg side kick because, defensively and offensively, I consider it to be the strongest. It is the safest kick and one of the most powerful kicks. When executed properly, it can be just as fast as the front kick, which is often considered the fastest kick of all. Therefore, when I teach combinations, I generally place emphasis on the lead hand and lead leg coupled with a great initial move.

### Range

The closer you get to your opponent, the better your accuracy. My teacher, Bruce Lee, always said that a good puncher will beat a good kicker. I tend to agree and might add that a good wrestler can beat a good puncher. That's my philosophy for one simple reason: the closer I get to you, the more accurate I become. That's pretty simple logic. Also, you must always fight your opponent from the zone in which he is defensively the weakest. So, if I fight a puncher, I want to fight him outside his zone or in grappling range inside his strength. Along the same lines, I want to fight the grappler outside his zone, where I have punches and kicks at my disposal. And, of course, I would want to fight the kicker inside his zone. That's a very basic strategy.

To recap, the initial move is crucial to the principles behind a combination. You want to explode. To accomplish this, I like to start the majority of my combinations with the lead leg and lead foot. I use the lead hand and the lead leg as tools to help me approach my opponent by enabling me to measure the distance—to help me get set before I unload the power or finishing technique. You must strive to do this also.

### COMBINATIONS

Working with co-author Jerry Beasley, Lewis demonstrates a basic combination training exercise that combines the low block with the lead-hand strike (figures 109–112).

FIGURE 109

FIGURE 110

FIGURE 111

FIGURE 112

FIGURE113

FIGURE 114

Here, the authors practice the counter side kick against the lead-hand strike (figures 113–115).

FIGURE 115

**57**

FIGURE 116

FIGURE 117

FIGURE 118

FIGURE 119

Lewis demonstrates the lead-hand strike (Figures 116–117) with the set-up reverse punch (figure 118), then changes leads to complete the reverse punch (figure 119).

In the next sequence, Lewis demonstrates some of the footwork that has made Joe Lewis American Karate Systems world famous. From the on-guard position (figure 120), Lewis draws the

FIGURE 120

FIGURE 121

FIGURE 122

FIGURE 123

opponent with a jab (figure 121), then fakes a reverse punch (figures 122–123) and finishes with the back fist (figure 124). With the proper footwork, Lewis can bridge the gap faster than his opponent can react to the first strike.

FIGURE 124

FIGURE 125

FIGURE 126

FIGURE 127

FIGURE 128

FIGURE 129

Here, Lewis initiates an upper body fake (figures 125-126), followed by a lower body fake (figure 127). The combination of two fast feints disrupts the opponent's rhythm, allowing Lewis to easily score with the back fist (figures 128-129).

FIGURE 130

FIGURE 131

FIGURE 132

FIGURE 133

Continuing with the lower body fake (figures 130–131), Lewis draws his opponent's guard low with a fake round kick (figure 132), which makes it easy for Lewis to connect with the back fist (figure 133).

FIGURE 134

FIGURE 135

FIGURE 136

FIGURE 137

Here, Lewis draws his opponent's defenses low (figures 134–135) and connects with a high hook kick (figures 136–137).

FIGURE 138

FIGURE 139

FIGURE 140

FIGURE 141

Using the lower body fake (figures 138–140), Lewis again finds an opening for the lead hand (figure 141) and, to finish the combination, buries a side kick into the opponent's unprotected rib cage (figure 142).

FIGURE 142

FIGURE 143

FIGURE 144

FIGURE 145

In this sequence, Lewis immobilizes his opponent with a stunning side kick to the hip to counter a lead jab (figures 143–145), then finishes the combination with a lead strike of his own (figures 146–147).

FIGURE 146

FIGURE 147

At right, Lewis begins his combination with a jab (figures 148–149), then follows with a front kick (figure 150) and a reverse punch (figure 151).

FIGURE 148

FIGURE 149

FIGURE 150

FIGURE 151

**67**

FIGURE 152

FIGURE 153

FIGURE 154

FIGURE 155

This time, Lewis draws his opponent into firing the jab (figures 152–153). Lewis steps out of the line of fire and delivers a counter side kick (figure 154) and a ridge hand (figure 155).

FIGURE 156

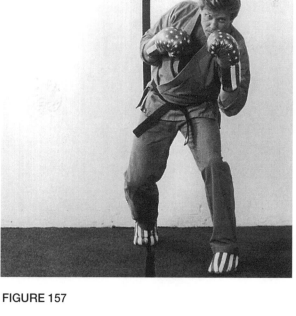

FIGURE 157

In this sequence, Lewis demonstrates the footwork that is the hallmark of the JLAKS style by employing the scramble step and body lean (figures 156–160), followed by a jab (figure 161) and a return to on guard (figure 162). JLAKS is best described by constant motion; the footwork best illustrates this.

FIGURE 158

FIGURE 159

FIGURE 160

FIGURE 161

FIGURE 162

FIGURE 163

Against opponent John Graden (right), Lewis draws a side kick (figures 163–164), then shuffles out of the way and quickly bridges the gap with a lead-hand strike (figures 165–166).

FIGURE 164

FIGURE 165

FIGURE 166

FIGURE 167

In this sequence, Lewis' constant shifting and footwork cause his opponent to miss the kick (figures 167–169), which allows Lewis to find an opening for his reverse punch (figure 170).

FIGURE 168

FIGURE 169

FIGURE 170

# CHAPTER FOUR

## Final Thoughts from Joe Lewis

**THE CONCEPT OF THE ULTIMATE WARRIOR**

By definition, I doubt that there could ever be an ultimate warrior. Everyone has at least one or two inadequacies that would disqualify him from ultimate warrior status. I think such a person exists only in fantasy, not unlike Batman, Superman, and other such heroes found only in the comics. If I were to attempt to create the imaginary ultimate warrior, obviously he would have to possess the basics: superior technique or weapons, unsurpassed physical attributes, and, of course, heart—the backbone and passion of one's fighting spirit. Without these basics, he would lack the ultimate mental toughness or that air of ring savvy, which fighters like the late Joe Louis and legendary Muhammad Ali possessed. I would prefer to give a psychological cross section of this individual than discuss his physical attributes or how well equipped he may be with techniques. I think herein lies one of the keys, that is, the strength in this warrior's disposition—his fighting attitude. You have to go beyond being properly prepared, armed, and equipped for an all-out open and total conflict. You must go beyond the mere struggle of ordinary physical combat

Joe Lewis sparring with Rocky Graziano on Hill 321 above Da Nang, 1965.

and beyond being pugnacious and game. When it comes to dealing with his opponents, the ultimate warrior knows how to quickly render his opponent's offense ineffective while capitalizing on his opponent's defensive weaknesses.

The warrior goes about this process with an eagerness to fight. He's one who likes to prolong the conflict. He can be dreadfully belligerent one moment and play opossum the next in order to gain the upper hand. He faces danger and suffers hardship resolutely. He does so almost as if he lacks the capacity to expect or even recognize impending danger, and yet he still can maintain the ability to effectively apply his knowledge regardless of his emotional involvement.

Joe knocked out Ronnie Barkoot in the first round of the 1971 Kickboxing Championships.

## The Mind as a Weapon

The key word that comes to mind when I think of the ultimate warrior is *intimidation*. I'm speaking of psychological intimidation. He maintains an intense, sustained quality of intimidation almost as if his mere intentions could cause the average fighter to yield. In short, when you confront the ultimate warrior, don't expect to be hurt; expect to be punished.

In addition to his psychological virtues, the ultimate warrior must possess other attributes. First is a sense of need. To me, a warrior lives not for money or glory, but for honor. He's not a heroic machine or a martyr for a cause, nor does he need to be supported by popular opinion. I would say that a portion of his deeds lends honor to his cause. The ultimate warrior might die in combat, but his image lives on. (I might admire his efforts, but not necessarily revere his motives or his cause.) The ultimate warrior is one who shapes and controls the battle. The circumstances of the battle do not dictate his actions.

Cuss D'Amada, the late trainer of Mike Tyson and a number of other world champions, including Floyd Patterson, used to say that "the ultimate in combat is to hit your opponent without being hit yourself." Bruce Lee liked this statement and often used it. I can't think of a more simple overview in describing what the ultimate is in combat.

I would go on to say that the ultimate warrior must be prudent in carrying out his strategy. The key to controlling your opponent is to be able to eliminate his advantage or destroy his advantage— to be able to render an opponent helpless by diminishing his strengths. These include speed, reach, aggressiveness, experience, size, and power. If you do this, everything else tends to collapse.

### Don't Get Hit

Let's go back to the first cardinal rule in fighting: *don't get hit*. The easiest way to accomplish this is by concentrating on denying your opponent access to the target at all times, while maintaining a strong defensive posture. In effect, you give your opponent as small a target as possible and never give him a stationary target. Stay out of his line of fire by relocating your position and therefore his target. In other words, know how to break ground or maneuver so that you are always varying the distance and alignment between you and your opponent. Ultimately, you don't want to be in his line of fire (what is often called the opponent's defensive perimeter).

### Neutralization

The second cardinal rule in fighting has to do with the most fundamental principle in fighting, which is to *neutralize your opponent's position before you attack*. You must make sure that your opponent's position is always weak and that your position is strong at the moment you choose to attack. The easiest way to accomplish this is to master the ability to prevent your opponent from getting set to fire against you. Of course, you must learn how to best set up against him so that you can fire at him when he is in a position of weakness, or when his position is in transition from one set-up to another. It all comes down to one faculty that most fighters seem to lack, and that is what I call mental toughness. Simply put, it's learning how to outthink your opponent.

### Fear and Intimidation

Mental intimidation, I've always thought, is the ultimate in combat; you must seize the offensive. It means negating fear, anger, and any other self-defeating behavior. Fear is an emotional state that is self-developed. In other words, what you see must be interpreted in your mind. Based on your experience, you may choose to visualize an opponent as frightening, undesirable, helpless, or any number of adjectives. You must learn to harness your fears and allow them to work *for* you. If you don't or can't do this, fear will handcuff your offense and collapse your defense.

Joe fighting Chuck Norris for the 1967 International Championship title. Steve Armstrong was the referee. Chuck was a great champion.

There is a saying in baseball that if you can't beat them with a bat, beat them with a glove. Sometimes you go up against an opponent who doesn't have an extremely good offense, but who might have an incredible defense. In the middle of the match you realize that you can't hit your opponent; your offense is basically useless. You become apprehensive and doubtful as to whether the tide is going to turn and whether your opponent is going to start testing *your* defense. Fear can set in, making you so blind that you can't even see your opponent's techniques coming at you. You lose the ability to focus. As you become totally involved with your inabilities and apprehension, fear can build and get completely out of hand, making you unable to focus properly on your

**BILL WALLACE**
Middle Weight Karate Champion

**JOE LEWIS**
World Heavyweight Karate Champion

Joe and Bill "Superfoot" Wallace sparring. Bill's kicking ability was a great factor in intimidating his opponent. His punch was equally devastating.

strategy. Fear of being hurt, of not being able to sustain the struggle, and of losing or looking bad, can result from poor focus. Fear also can take your breath away because you become tight and breathe in a shallow manner; your muscles tense up, you're not as quick, and you become mentally apprehensive. Fear allows your opponent to detect your intentions and read your body language, which may allow him to make the process of addressing you with his offense a lot easier.

There is an old story in the fight game: two opposing fighters are in their respective dressing rooms before the fight and the word spreads that one of the fighters can't get his gloves on. A fearful person might think, "Oh, his hands are too big for the gloves." Actually, the fighter is so afraid that he can't bring himself to allow the gloves to be placed on his hands.

There are a number of tests that you can use in your training sessions to prepare yourself for dealing with fear, and all fears can be dealt with. I've always felt that the fear of feeling and looking inadequate is a factor more so than the fear of losing or being hurt, but sometimes there is the fear of making mistakes, too. If you don't make mistakes, you won't learn anything. In fact, I believe that there is no such thing as a mistake. The term *mistake* is just another word for a process of transition, of learning. When you make a mistake, it's a way of teaching yourself what not to do the next time. Remember, fear is self-developed and self-defeating. It is also self-controlled. As Walter Anderson points out in *The Confidence Course*, success is nothing more than a long list of mistakes until you finally get it right.

## Physical Toughness

One of the big differences between point fighters and full-contact fighters is the ability to take punishment. How tough is your body? Can you not only hit hard but also take a hard shot to the chin or gut? It's not just an important factor, it's a critical one. According to top fight promoters, nine out of 10 fighters have glass jaws. I believe that percentage could be greatly decreased if fighters worked on toughening their bodies. When I was in the Marine Corps, I once talked to some young men who were going through Officer Candidate School (OCS) and I remember one of the lessons they had learned: one of the first rules in learning how to become an officer in the Marine Corps is to be able to take orders; if you can't take an order, don't expect to be able to give one.

The same principle holds true in the fight game. If you can't take the punishment, don't expect to be able to deal it out. Learn to take it first; be able to sustain the pain. Not being able to take the pain will result immediately in a loss of focus. A number of fighters, upon receiving a hard blow to the midsection, will back off. They fall down or run to the corner. In a state of panic, they lose control because they have not been taught to be mentally tough in such a situation. When you get hit, don't focus on the pain, focus on the game. The game is the opponent in front of you—what he's trying to do to you and what you're trying to keep him from doing to you. You've got to stick with your strategy. You've got to focus.

Although I seldom use the term *Bushido*, I suppose we each have a moral code. I've never been in trouble in my life over any kind of physical encounters or violence. There are two principles that I have heard during my lifetime that reflect this fact: I believe in "an eye for an eye" and "do unto others as you would have them do unto you." I know that my well being, my welfare, and my life aren't here to allow another person to attack, strike, or abuse me, and likewise I feel that respect must be mutual. I don't condone violence; I despise it when I hear about it or when I see parents striking their children for any reason.

Emotionally, it depends on the context as to what my code of ethics or system of principles and rules would be in governing a particular situation. My gut reaction is, if you hit me, I'll probably hit you back. If you kick my dog, I'll probably do more than that. I always trust my thinking processes and I know that I'll do the right thing. I'm not known as the kind of person who would call the police or yell for help. If a person is angry with me for some reason, I believe that the first thing to do is to try to diffuse the anger before acting, whether acting verbally or physically, even though it's hard to determine in advance what would realistically take place when making a moral decision in a survival situation. You're brought up to believe that you're not supposed to hit other people. Therefore, you don't feel comfortable when in the act of harming others. If you are physically attacked and you don't do anything to defend yourself, short of dying, there is a lot of suffering you could go through. You might feel bad about yourself because you didn't do anything when you should have. On the other hand, if you do something to defend yourself and you're successful, you may feel bad because you struck back or struck in such a way as to incapacitate the person. You may feel morally wrong and may be in some sort of legal jeopardy. I believe, however, that there are times in such vehemently violent situations—when your life is threatened or your welfare is in great jeopardy—that spoken moral codes have little meaning. You must survive using whatever means you have available. It's irrational to judge one's moral behavior in a crisis situation.

In the boxing gym, there is the old saying, *don't be first and don't be second*. That means do not go out there and throw the first punch because it's morally wrong, and when we say don't be second, it means that if you get fired on first, don't be the second one to land your punch. I use that saying when teaching. Other gyms have the saying, *be quick, be first, and don't stop*. (I kind of like that one.) One that we used when I was on Okinawa was *never quit*. It's hard to be beaten up if you never quit.

I think of myself as a martial artist first—not as a fighter—and as a martial artist, everything is defensive. My fighting strategy is defensive and every kata in martial arts starts off in the defensive. I analyze all of my opponents from a defensive point of view first. My concluding remark on the subject of defense is that if you strike me first, I may not forgive you for striking me, but I will forgive you if you can't hit me as hard as I may hit you back.

Everything I have discussed so far has been based on personal experience. I've been physically attacked a couple of times in my life, and every time (being that I'm a choke artist), I simply choked the aggressor unconscious in no time flat. My knockouts usually come with the application of the choke hold. As I place my forearm in a striking manner around the neck, I hit the carotid sinus just below the ear lobe or the brachial plexus and, more than 60 percent of the time when I applied the choke hold in real self-defense situations, I subsequently knocked my opponents unconscious before I even began to apply the choke itself. When these people came to, I simply stood behind them where they couldn't bite, butt, kick, punch, or grab me. My hands were ready to quickly render them unconscious again if necessary, although I've never been in a situation in which I had to follow through with a second choke hold. Usually, when they wake up, their anger and nonsense has dissipated.

I do have a fear of striking somebody for real. I'm afraid that if I really let loose, my power could immediately kill a person. That's why I don't strike people. I usually just grab their hair and pull them off balance until they calm down, or I choke them out. This always has seemed to work for me when it was impossible to avoid the situation. I wouldn't want to wish any sort of predicament of this nature on anyone. I might add that just being a black belt in martial arts does not give anyone a license or a degree of immunity to believe that they are omnipotent enough to always steer free of the situation or handle it. I have personally seen just as many black belts get their butts beaten in street fights as I have seen black belts win.

▼

There are simply too many variables to predict the outcome of a fight. So how do we develop a fighting concept for the ultimate warrior?

All competitive events, including self-defense, are determined by a combination of strategy, attributes, and chance (luck). One may train for the ultimate strategy and develop the ultimate attributes, yet both can be negated by chance. Nonetheless, chance can be dictated to some degree by selecting the right martial art.

## CHOOSING BETWEEN TRADITIONAL AND NONTRADITIONAL MARTIAL ARTS

Can a martial artist ever be sufficiently trained and wise enough to know what is best for another, whether traditional or nontraditional martial arts? I don't think so. Look around and you will discover many formulas for what combination of skills, strategies, and attitudes makes a great martial artist. Because we are all unique individuals, no one system or style can ever be best for everyone. Qualities from each school of thought must inevitably coexist in each of us.

Martial arts traditionalists choose to conform without question to established practices and styles passed down through generations. Early in my career, however, I began a gradual break from this point of view, for a variety of reasons. First, coming into the martial arts from the fitness and weightlifting world, I soon discovered that traditional schools knew very little about the overall development of athletes. While cardiovascular development, strength, and flexibility always have been the three major aspects of physical training, it was impossible to find a good balance of these in the martial arts. In addition, a number of questions surfaced for me which could not be sufficiently dealt with by those devoted to traditional training.

Joe in a fight scene from *Jaguar Lives*. (175): Barbara Bach stared in *Jaguar Lives* with Joe, along with Christopher Lee. (176): Joe dropped to 180 pounds for the filming of *Jaguar Lives*. (Photos 175-177: Copyright 1979 by American International Pictures.)

For example, look at the side straddle stance and the way traditionalists teach us to place our fists in the inverted position next to our hips. I have always felt that it would be difficult to move quickly from this position. Why would I want my fists held in a position to protect my hips, with elbows stuck out behind me? It always seemed to make more sense to keep my hands in front of my face, my elbows in front of my ribs, and to stand in a way that would allow me to move in either direction with equal speed, as well as equal skill.

Other questions troubled me. Why were there no body movements during sparring or even during tactical self-defense drills? For example, we never did any feints or fakes. We never ducked, bobbed, or wove. We never rocked back and forth with the body or did any piking motions. There were no footwork drills (in particular, no sliding off to the right or left on an angle) and no lateral footwork. When we did attacking drills, why did we always have to stand directly in front of the attacker? This doesn't make sense if you are facing someone bigger who is more experienced and more aggressive.

We were taught how to punch and kick. However, there was little or no training in how to *set up* our favorite techniques. What is the best way to bridge the gap between you and your opponent? How can you best "squeeze the trigger" so that the moment you move off the firing line, you are explosive as well as deceptive? How can you camouflage your initial move so that your opponent finds it difficult to read you? How do you deal with an opponent who is bigger, faster, taller, or more aggressive than you? How can you smother an opponent's speed or keep him off balance so that he cannot use his size or reach against you? What is the tactical difference between dealing with a quick lead-off fighter versus dealing with a sly counterfighter? Do you fight a good puncher differently than a good kicker? How do you shake someone's mind-set when he has more experience than you (thus eliminating his advantage)? What is the difference between a technique, a tactic, and a strategy, and at what point do I employ each in the interest of controlling either my opponent or the situation between us? How do I incorporate my body weight and my emotions to give my executions more conviction, real backbone, and effectiveness? How do I tap into that crucial element known as my own *fighting spirit*? How can I learn to read my opponent so that I can most effectively adjust to his game plan? These are just a few of the many questions that occurred to me over the years.

The language barrier between those of us in the United States and our original instructors from Asia was a challenge. What I realized over time, however, was that even those who did master the English language had no answers to questions like these. Therefore, their philosophical ascendants had no answers for me, either.

Elementary psychology tells us that the level of a person's self-esteem and confidence is directly reflected in what that individual does. Likewise, one's actions in the ring or in a fight are a reflection of actions within the mind, and this means that answers to questions like those posed here, regarding mental processes and attitudes, are crucial to achieving excellence in the martial arts.

In the beginning, all martial artists are taught a number of old-fashioned, outdated maneuvers. Being novices at first, they naturally accept these premises as truth and, over time, may become attached to them. It is when we close our eyes to evidence that is telling us that we are mistaken that we find ourselves in trouble.

For example, if you have been taught to execute a karate punch and, when you pull the punch to its starting position, your forearm or fist ends up protecting your hip instead of your ribcage or face, then it should be self-evident that what you have been taught is impractical. If you stubbornly continue to execute the punch the same way, your loyalty is not to truth or practicality, but rather to the darkness your instructor prescribes. When we allow ourselves to become overattached to these old positions, our consciousness shrinks and our training becomes misguided. The end result is damaged self-esteem, such that we no longer have the confidence to move with conviction or execute to our highest level.

Over the years, I have noticed that a lack of inner security often breeds an emotional need to be unified with a traditional system. You must remember that *individuals create styles and systems*. The converse should not hold true; styles never should make individuals. Many styles have been lost or forgotten, but great individuals are never forgotten. For example, we may forget the precise significance of the theory of relativity, but we never will forget Albert Einstein. We may forget the significance of Bruce Lee's jeet kune do, but we never will forget Bruce.

It is my strong feeling that spontaneity and expression of self are important elements in one's growth as a martial artist. Does your system control you, or do you control the system? When you are being controlled, you cannot express freely. A free-choice, non-traditional system gives people more responsibility for their own actions. Their techniques, tactics, teaching methods, and training routines are tested openly. They are not confined to testing only against a prescribed style, with the absence of any unpredictable elements. Testing openly also eliminates the outdated notion that traditional practices and skills cannot be improved. I always tell my black belts to get into the ring and see if they can make anything work other than their mouths.

Many traditional protocols are seemingly breached by the JLAKS stylists. For example, a JLAKS stylist will use a great deal of lateral movement. When he trains, he bobs, weaves, fakes, and uses more lead-hand and lead-leg set-up strikes. He also uses the rear hand rather than the front hand for defense. Perhaps he will not practice the use of old farm tools as weapons, do the old katas, or wear the all-white gi.

When you do something that is nonoffensive and you do it because you like it, *that* should be your top priority, not the fact that you feel a need to subscribe to a set of inflexible, traditional rules. Just because you wear a dark-colored gi (which, by the way, makes it strategically more difficult for an opponent to read your moves, and is less likely to become stained and discolored), wear gloves at your karate school, mix grappling in with karate instruction, or use background music, does not mean that you are showing contempt for anyone's traditional values. Sometimes tradition works and sometimes it does not. You are doing it because you like it. It is simply no one else's business.

When people come into the martial arts, they do not come expecting an instructor to mold and fit them into some kind of cocoon. They want to be shown how to come out of the cocoon. People come in order to grow and be energized, to be drawn out of themselves. *To develop*. Martial arts never should be a process of rote imitation or emulation. At its best, it is an art form with the purpose of showing a person how to develop from within and to express his or her unique individuality.

Generally, there is a great deal of complacency in traditional martial arts schools, and often one school will polarize itself against another for whatever reason. Often, there is even deception going on in the form of making claims that are simply untrue, and instructors are seldom really fine-tuned or spend time upgrading their skills and knowledge. There is typically an attitude of, *well, this is what I was taught, so I will pass it on to you, and you pass me the money*. These kinds of attitudes make martial arts stagnant and essentially uncreative.

For me, as the founder of JLAKS, I had a grass-roots mandate, a vision, and a purpose. I began by asking myself the question, *am I a credit or a discredit to the martial arts?* I trusted my instincts and embraced an ambitious goal: to develop and promote a style that would become the standard by which all other styles are judged.

For this attitude and goal I have paid a price. Over the years, magazines and various instructors, feeling threatened, have tried to discredit me and my training partners. I would ask my detractors one question: does it follow that, by seeking to discredit me, the stature of your own style is enhanced? The old saying, *he who angers you, conquers you*, applies here. My feeling is that every minute you spend angry or envious of another martial artist or his style is one minute less that you are going to spend happy or creating something worthwhile with your own training; one minute less that you could spend motivating someone to become credible in your own style; one minute less that you could spend making yourself look better. Instead of looking at something new as a break from tradition, and therefore bad and untrustworthy, try looking at it as an opportunity to explore something creative that may work even better.

In my case, I would ask that you consider the record. As a JLAKS stylist and nontraditionalist, I became the first martial artist to win world championships in two different sports: karate and kickboxing. Honors have come consistently throughout my career, including my being voted into several halls of fame. The point here is not to turn the spotlight on me personally, but to make a point, i.e., that there must be something basically correct and worthy about the thinking that has made all these accomplishments possible.

JLAKS stylists seek to acquire savvy in their executions as well as consistency. These are two of the highest compliments you could ever pay another martial artist. We seek to give students the know-how and the experience to manipulate or outmaneuver various opponents by using tactics, strategies, and superior mind-sets, which are not taught in traditional styles. Based on the student's experience and training, everything he does will arise out of experimentation and critical observation, not mere tradition. When he is in the ring or engaged in training, he is like a scientist on the cutting edge of research, with his thinking *rooted in, but not bound by, the best knowledge currently available*. He does not rely solely on tradition, on what has come before, which, in the case of martial arts in the United States, includes a great deal of heresy and nonsense, much of which has

1990 World Champion Karate College instructors: L-R: Jerry Beasley, Jeff Smith, Bill Wallace, and Joe Lewis.

been passed on by those who have never really trained or fought. What he relies on instead is creative experimentation; what actually works in the situation at hand versus what doesn't.

Therefore, the key differences between the JLAKS stylist and the traditionalist are 1) the constitution of their training habits and 2) the psychology to which they subscribe. More than someone who acquires the mere mechanical skills of a martial art, the JLAKS stylist learns how to think. He develops a philosophy—a training constitution—and a set of internally generated practices that gradually but effectively bring about a fundamental change in the healthiest way possible. This change is primarily characterized by the development and intentional use of a stronger self-esteem and personal confidence, which helps him achieve, among other things, success in the martial arts. Chiefly, it is this kind of focus on individual self-reliance and development that separates us from the traditionalists.

For the hard-core traditionalist who switches over to the JLAKS style, the change can feel almost miraculously liberating and lead to much greater success in his discipline. Once his strong preconditioning wears off, we begin to see a merging of knowledge and personality that leads to execution characterized by spontaneity and conviction.

*Spontaneity with conviction*—this is the credo of the Joe Lewis American Karate Systems martial artist—an attitude that can make one invincible, not in mere technique or in flesh, but in spirit.

# About the Authors

JOE LEWIS began studying martial arts in the Marine Corps when stationed on Okinawa in 1964. He earned his first black belt in only seven months' time. After serving in Vietnam, he trained with the legendary Bruce Lee for more than a year. Joe created American full-contact karate/kickboxing in 1970 and later founded the Joe Lewis American Karate Systems. He has been inducted into 12 martial arts halls of fame, has won more major tournaments than any other martial artist in history, and his contributions to American karate have been so significant that he was called "The Greatest Karate Fighter of All Time." Joe can be contacted for appearances and JLAKS information at PO Box 3322, Wilmington, NC 28406 (tel. 800-365-4748).

DR. JERRY BEASLEY, a professor at Radford University, is considered America's foremost collegiate martial arts educator. A professor at Radford University, his office has become a virtual martial arts laboratory. Having earned both his master's and doctoral degrees (in part for his thesis and dissertation in martial arts) from Virginia Tech, Beasley is in the unique position of being able to combine his scientific research methodologies with more than 30 years of martial arts study. Beasley, a two-time American All-Star taekwon do champion (1975-76), is the only person to have received the 8th dan in Joe Lewis' American Karate Systems. Beasley has authored two additional Paladin Press books and more than 100 articles in leading martial arts journals.